Original title:
Rhyme Among the Roots

Copyright © 2025 Creative Arts Management OÜ
All rights reserved.

Author: Seraphina Caldwell
ISBN HARDBACK: 978-1-80567-170-1
ISBN PAPERBACK: 978-1-80567-469-6

Verse of the Verdure

In the garden, veggies dance,
With carrots prancing, taking a chance.
Tomatoes giggle, red as a clown,
While lettuce fluffs in its leafy gown.

Onions swaying, shedding their tears,
Claiming they're brave over countless years.
Potatoes roll, playing hide and seek,
In muddy puddles, they're blissfully chic.

Spinach spies, perched high on a stem,
Whispers of mischief, and then a gem.
Radishes chuckle, bright little dots,
In the soil's embrace, they plot and plot.

But when the chef arrives with a knife,
The veggies gasp at the cutthroat life!
Yet laughter echoes with every slice,
In the pot, they bounce, how nice, how nice!

Verse Veils of the Vines

In a garden full of giggles,
The vines twist like a pair of wiggles.
They tangle and dance, oh what a sight,
Giggling leaves in the warm sunlight.

A snail in a race moves oh so slow,
While frogs below put on a show.
With jumps and hops, they steal the scene,
A froggy troupe in bright shades of green.

A worm with jokes that burrow deep,
Makes the flowers chuckle, laugh, and leap.
Their petals sway with a laugh or two,
Blooming bright in colors so true.

As bees buzz in a playful chase,
Each flower tries to win the race.
With pollen sprinkles and nectar sips,
These garden tales bring funny quips.

Cadence in the Clusters

In the bunch where berries play,
They argue loudly about the day.
A cherry claims she's the sweetest prize,
While a grape just rolls his tiny eyes.

Lemons giggle at the grape's old tale,
Citrus jokes that never fail.
Their peels of laughter fill the air,
As prunes chime in, 'Life's only fair!'

An apple grins with shining skin,
While pears wheeze softly from within.
Their chatter grows ripe, a funny sound,
Blessed by humor all around.

Dancing about in fruity glee,
They tiptoe on branches, wild and free.
With every sway, they twist and spin,
A cluster fest where fun begins.

Sonorous Shadows of the Saplings

Little saplings strut and sway,
Whispering jokes as they play.
Their shadows stretch far and wide,
Tickling the roots that hide inside.

A dandelion shouts a pun,
Says, 'I'm the lightest—look how I run!'
But the oak shakes its leafy head,
'You float away, but I'm still fed!'

The birch pranks with a rustle or two,
'Watch me dance like I'm brand new!'
While laughter echoes in forest halls,
Even the rocks can echo their brawls.

Each sapling brings a silly cheer,
Their woodland dance makes sadness disappear.
In every flap and leafy prance,
The shadows sing a merry dance.

Prose of the Petals

Petals flutter like pages bright,
Reading tales of sheer delight.
With colors bold and whispers sweet,
They pen a story on their feet.

A daisy declares its flower power,
While tulips plot in every hour.
Their prose contains a giggle or two,
Of bees that buzz and don't know what to do.

A rose with thorns, so sharp yet proud,
Cracks jokes that draw a curious crowd.
Amid the blooms, the laughter wakes,
And every petal shares what it takes.

At dusk, when the garden sighs and yawns,
The prose continues, as laughter dawns.
Each blossom joins in the gentle bets,
Who's the funniest in the flower sets?

Ballad of the Blossoms

In a garden where daisies dance,
Bees are buzzing, lost in a trance.
Tulips twirl with silly glee,
Winking at clouds, just wait and see.

Butterflies join the merry race,
Flitting around with silly grace.
Petals giggle in the sun's warm light,
Making the flowers feel just right.

A daffodil jokes with a rose so grand,
Telling tales of a far-off land.
They chuckle as the daisies tease,
Oh what fun among the breeze!

And if you listen close, you'll hear,
Laughter floating, crystal clear.
Nature's humor, fresh and bright,
In blooms that giggle with delight.

Poetry of the Pine Cones

Pine cones gather, all in a bunch,
Talking secrets over lunch.
"Who's the tallest?" one asks with glee,
"Not me!" shouts a fir from the tree!

Squirrels giggle, their tails up high,
Watching the cones spin and try.
"Roll like we mean it!" they cheer with pride,
As one cone tumbles down the slide.

A wise old spruce shares quite the tale,
Of a brave pine cone that wore a veil.
"Did it fly?" the young ones inquire,
"Nah," he laughs, "just rolled in the fire!"

As night falls, they nestle tight,
Whispering jokes, what a sight!
In the forest, filled with laughter,
The pine cones celebrate happily ever after.

Serenade of the Scented Woods

In woods alive with scents divine,
Frogs croak rhymes over clinking wine.
"Moss is plush!" says one with flair,
"Did you see my new lounge chair?"

The flowers sway, they twirl along,
To the tunes of the crickets' song.
"More minty fresh than a gumdrop!"
Laughter rising, making hearts hop.

Trees share puns, their branches curved,
"Who's the best? I'm well-deserved!"
"Not without your roots, dear friend,"
The bark replies, "On me, depend."

Underneath stars, the giggles flow,
Mice march in a fanciful show.
In the scented woods, so grand and free,
Every laugh a sweet harmony.

Chronicles of the Clover Field

In a field of clovers, green and fair,
Ladybugs twirl, light as air.
"Hop along!" a grasshopper teases,
Count our jumps, show off our pleases!

Dandelions laugh, their heads held high,
Blowing wishes toward the sky.
"Tell me a joke!" calls out a bee,
"We're all ears, come giggle with me!"

A clover shouts, "I found a four-leaf!"
"What's your secret?" It's a fun motif!
"No clue, just luck!" comes the quick reply,
With chuckles and winks, oh my, oh my!

As the sun sets, they settle down,
No room for grumps, not a frown.
In the clover field, fun never yields,
Sharing stories, laughter builds.

Syllables in the Soil

In the garden, rabbits play,
Chasing shadows, what a day!
Worms are dancing, feeling spry,
Underneath the bluest sky.

Grumpy carrots wear a frown,
While the radishes spin 'round.
Beans are giggling up so high,
Swapping secrets, oh my my!

Parsnips tell the silliest tales,
As the broccoli wiggles, flails.
Tomatoes blush and turn so red,
When beetles try to steal their bed.

With each seed, the laughter grows,
In a patch where fun just flows.
Nature's humor blooms so bright,
In this garden, pure delight.

Murmurs of the Marigold

Marigolds gossip with the bees,
Whispering secrets on the breeze.
Daisies chuckle at the sun,
Poppy seeds say, "Let's have fun!"

Underneath the leafy crowd,
Silly stems rejoice aloud.
Petals prance in vibrant cheer,
While mischievous ants draw near.

Sunflowers grin at passing flies,
"Look at those! They're quite the spies!"
Every sprout shares a bright joke,
Even the stems give a poke!

Laughter lingers in the air,
Among the blooms without a care.
Nature plays its merry tune,
As flowers dance beneath the moon.

Stanzas from the Sprouts

Up in the garden, sprouts arise,
With photosynthesis in their eyes.
Lettuce sings and peppers hum,
"Let's all have a little fun!"

Radial rhymes wrap round the beans,
As kale bursts out in vibrant greens.
Zucchini tries its luck to sway,
But tripping on its leaves, hooray!

Cucumbers giggle, picking mates,
While pumpkins jovially contemplate.
Turnips star in their own play,
The veggies laugh and shout hooray!

Every sprout sprinkles smiles,
Joyful laughter stretches miles.
In this patch of leafy delight,
They share their dream of purest light.

Lyrics of Lost Landscapes

Once in a field where shadows blend,
A cabbage found an unlikely friend.
An old scarecrow with a crooked hat,
Giggled at crows, yelling, "How 'bout that?"

Beneath the soil, strange sounds arise,
Earthworms plotting, what a surprise!
They joke about their muddy plight,
Wishing for a sunny flight.

Flowers dance in a whimsical show,
While grasses sway to and fro.
"Let's write a song, let's be free!"
Sang a clover with glee, whee!

In landscapes lost, joy fills the air,
Funny echoes everywhere.
Nature's tune never goes stale,
In every leaf, there's a funny tale!

Harmony in the Hedges

A squirrel in the bushes sings,
He thinks he's found some golden rings.
With acorns stacked, he starts to prance,
In leafy hues, he takes a chance.

The hedgehogs laugh, they roll on by,
With little feet, they seem to fly.
They poke their heads, then jump and dive,
In this green world, they feel alive.

Murmurs of the Moss

Beneath the trees, the moss agrees,
To tickle toes in summer breeze.
The rabbits hop, they giggle loud,
In this soft home, they're feeling proud.

With tiny hats of dew on top,
The skinks parade, they dance and bop.
They whisper tales of muddy fun,
In secret spots, the games begun.

Dances in the Dahlia

The daisies spin in wild delight,
While butterflies join in the fight.
They flit and flutter, oh what a scene,
In colors bright, they're feeling keen.

The ladybugs, they join the dance,
A wiggly waltz, a clumsy prance.
With petals swirling, all aglow,
They laugh and cheer, what a show!

Rhapsody of the Rainfall

When raindrops fall like candy sprigs,
The puddles form, and frogs do jigs.
With little boots, they splash around,
In watery fun, their joys abound.

The worms emerge in vibrant cheer,
They wiggle out without a fear.
With laughter loud, the rivulets play,
As nature sings, come join the fray!

Verse of Verdant Valleys

In the valley where grass grows bright,
Bunnies hop and take to flight.
Squirrels sing with acorn hats,
Dancing round to chubby chats.

The flowers giggle, swaying so,
While bees hum tunes, in joyful flow.
A snail slips on his tiny shell,
And shouts, "Oh dear, I tripped! Oh well!"

The sunbeams play a game of tag,
While daisies hold their bowing brag.
Around the brook, frogs leap and glide,
As fish join in, like a wavy ride.

In this vale of tricks and jests,
Nature's laughter never rests.
With every rock and every root,
Life's a dance and oh, so cute!

Whispers in the Wilderness

In the woods where shadows play,
The foxes plot both night and day.
A raccoon nods, his mask so sly,
He steals your snacks, oh me, oh my!

The owls hoot in dulcet tones,
While woodpeckers beat like metronomes.
A bear breaks in for honey spreads,
Oh, sticky paws and messy beds!

Mice chirp gossip as they roam,
While crickets serenade their home.
The trees, they sway, with secrets grand,
As critters prance in merry band.

Whispers swirl upon the breeze,
Echoing through the dancing trees.
In this wild, whimsical domain,
Laughter lives where none complain!

Cadence of the Clover

In a patch of four-leaf glee,
Ladybugs dance with bumblebees.
Grasshoppers leap, with hops so bold,
Sharing tales that never get old.

The clovers twirl, a lively show,
While the ants march in a row.
One slips, and down they all tumble,
Creating a miniature jumble!

A worm pops up to say hello,
With dirt on his hat, he steals the show.
With every wiggle, he brings forth
A giggle fit, of massive worth.

In the brush, a rabbit prances,
Through hidden paths of funny chances.
In this land where chuckles bloom,
Every step is a lark, a zoom!

Notes from the Nestled Nook

In the nook where the shadows cling,
A squirrel's chattering takes wing.
With nuts piled high, he draws a map,
Of all the trees for a glorious nap.

A tiny owl in glasses peers,
Sipping tea with woodland cheers.
"A joke!" he says with a winkle gaze,
"Why did the acorn cross the maze?"

The answer flits like birds in flight,
"To get to the roots of pure delight!"
With sighs and smiles, they share their tales,
As laughter dances on gentle gales.

In this nook where mischief brews,
The whispers tickle every muse.
So come and join this joyous crook,
In the warm embrace of the nestled nook!

Symphony of the Subtle Sprouts

In the garden, a snail did sing,
A tune so slow, it missed the spring.
The daisies danced, with petals bright,
While worms wore hats, a charming sight.

Beneath the leaves, the ants would play,
On tiny drums, they'd start their day.
Beetles curled, like marbles round,
With laughter echoing from the ground.

Resonance of the Rooted Realm

The roots below had quite a bash,
With laughter loud, and a loud crash.
A radish sneezed, it made quite a sound,
Like a trumpet from the underground.

The carrots jived, with tops held high,
While turnips tried their best to fly.
The soil shook, as all would cheer,
For veggie jokes were all we'd hear.

Whispers in the Undergrowth

Under bushes, secrets spread,
With gnomes in hats, that's what they said.
A toadstool prince was seen doing a jig,
While mushrooms giggled, all feeling big.

The crickets chirped their silly tunes,
As fireflies danced beneath the moons.
In this patch, where the green things twirl,
Every leaf holds laughter, in a whirl.

Echoes of the Earth

Beneath the soil, a party's call,
As roots and bugs had a ball.
The earthworms joked, with slippery grace,
While beetles donned a fancy lace.

Mossy mats became the floor,
Where flowers dipped and twirled for more.
The thrill of dirt, oh what a sight,
In underground waves, they danced all night.

Harmonies in the Hearth

The cozy flames dance with glee,
They crackle jokes, as warm as tea.
Pots and pans start to unwind,
With silly tunes, they're so entwined.

A spatula spins like a top,
While spoons perform a humorous hop.
In this kitchen, laughter's a part,
Where everyone's welcome, just take heart.

Lullabies of the Leaves

The leaves whisper secrets of the breeze,
Tickling squirrels who giggle with ease.
Every rustle brings a chuckle or two,
As branches sway, dancing just for you.

A twig dressed up in a fancy hat,
Begins to tease a passing fat cat.
Wind plays pranks, a playful jest,
In this foliage, it's laughter's nest.

Melodies of the Meadow

In the meadow, grasshoppers sing,
Twirling in circles like a bright spring.
Butterflies flutter, with style so grand,
Wearing polka dots, they take a stand.

A rabbit hops in a curtsy flare,
While daisies giggle without a care.
Together they weave a comedic tune,
Under the smile of a bouncing moon.

Ballads Beneath the Bark

Trees in concert, their voices blend,
With tales of squirrels they love to send.
The acorns chuckle, rolling down,
As chubby chipmunks steal the crown.

Beneath the bark, a joke takes root,
As nature's jesters raise a hoot.
With every ring, a memory spins,
In this forest, everyone grins.

Poetry of the Petals

In the garden, petals chat,
About the weather and the cat.
One says, 'I'm feeling quite blue!',
The sun shines bright, as if on cue.

A bee buzzed in, with laughs galore,
'Who ordered pollen by the score?'
The roses blushed, the daisies danced,
While tulips twirled, all quite entranced.

Lily pads giggle on the pond,
While frogs in bow ties sing their bond.
'Quack!' said the duck, 'I'm feeling grand!',
As petals soaked in sunlight's hand.

But then the wind came, oh so sly,
It teased the petals, made them fly.
They swirled around, a petal show,
And landed soft, with a gentle glow.

Tones of the Timber

In the forest, trees share tales,
Of squirrels' mischief and fox's trails.
Oak laughs loud, with a booming sound,
While birch whispers secrets around.

A crow caws jokes from high above,
He tells of a mouse who fell in love.
The pines sway gently, keepin' up,
With giggling leaves, their laughter's sup.

Beneath the boughs, where shadows creep,
A chipmunk hops, then takes a leap.
He slips on acorns, rolls with glee,
A comedy show for you and me.

Amid the trunks, the banter flows,
With bark's wise cracks, as each one knows.
The forest hums a playful tune,
As nature's jesters welcome June.

Comunions in the Canopy

Up in the branches, birds convene,
Discussing snacks and the latest scene.
One boasts of seeds he found today,
While others chirp in a funny way.

A magpie strutted, all dressed in black,
'Who borrowed my nest?' he gave a clack.
A sparrow giggled, 'Not me, dear chap!
I'm too busy napping, maybe a nap!'

The canopy sways with laughter and cheer,
As owls roll eyes, "Why are we here?"
In dusk's soft glow, they share a toast,
To friendships true, that matter most.

Then came a gust, the chatter's tossed,
'Who left the door open, we're all quite lost!'
With a flap and a flutter, the boughs grow bold,
As feathers mingle, stories unfold.

Songbirds in the Sycamore

In the sycamore, the songbirds play,
With tunes so bright, they dance all day.
One twirled high, on a swaying branch,
While others gave a little prance.

A wren sings sweet, while magpies tease,
They dive and dash with the greatest ease.
'I'll bet a worm that I can fly!'
Said the finch with a chirp, almost shy.

The branches sway with their winged frolic,
As nature laughs, it's simply symbolic.
But watch out now, for a hawk's near,
They scatter and whistle, filled with cheer.

They hide in leaves, from eyes so keen,
Then pop back out, all safe and unseen.
In the sycamore's arms, they sing bright,
With joyful tunes that take to flight.

Echoes Beneath the Evergreens

Beneath the pines, the squirrels play,
   Chasing shadows, funny ballet.
A chipmunk slips on pinecone grand,
   Falls with flair, the clumsy stand.

   The owls hoot in a silly way,
   Critiquing how the rabbits sway.
They wink and nod, all in good fun,
The forest laughs with each little pun.

   A raccoon wearing a tiny hat,
   Wanders near, quite clever and fat.
   With every step, a twirl and spin,
The woods erupt, let the giggles begin.

Among the roots, the laughter flows,
   Echoing where the sunshine glows.
In this green realm, hilarity grows,
   A world where joy forever glows.

Serenades in the Sagebrush

In the sagebrush, the lizards dance,
With little moves that enhance their chance.
A cactus poses, proud and stout,
While tumbleweeds just twirl about.

A jackrabbit plays a cheeky tune,
Underneath a silver moon.
He hops around, quite spry and keen,
Declaring each leaf a marionette queen.

The wrens chirp in harmonious glee,
As they gossip 'bout the bee in the tree.
A sagebrush serenade takes flight,
With each verse, it feels so light.

In the desert, they giggle and cheer,
The sun shines bright, the sky is clear.
These humorous notes, they love to sing,
In the sagebrush, let joy take wing.

Prose from the Pollen

The bees buzz with a poet's flair,
Crafting verses in the fragrant air.
Each pollen grain, a word they weave,
In blossoms bright, they never leave.

A bumblebee trips on his own feet,
While trying to find a flower sweet.
He shakes his head, what a silly plight,
Yet finds a bloom, oh what a sight!

The daisies giggle, laughing loud,
As they spy on the clumsy crowd.
A sunflower joins, tall and grand,
Waving its petals, a quirky band.

In this garden of prose and glee,
Nature's humor sets us free.
With every buzz and flutter around,
Life's little joys are truly found.

Rhapsody of the Roots

The roots below, they twist and twine,
Whispers echo with a silly line.
Worms tell jokes beneath the ground,
The laughter bounces all around.

A gopher pops up, laughs in surprise,
With a messy tuft of grass for disguise.
He winks and nods, in underground glee,
As branches tickle, such harmony!

The laughter flows like gentle streams,
As fungi giggle, sharing dreams.
With every wiggle, every shake,
Joyful roots can never break.

In this world, the fun ignites,
With silly songs and merry sights.
A rhapsody beneath our feet,
In nature's heart, our joys repeat.

Lyrics of the Latticework

In a garden filled with glee,
The plants seem to dance with tea.
Lettuce giggles at the sun,
While carrots race, oh what fun!

Peas are busy telling jokes,
While radishes play pranks on folks.
The flowers chuckle, swaying high,
As butterflies wave and fly by.

Tomatoes blush in the spotlight,
As they ripen, feeling just right.
Celery sings with a crunchy tone,
In this patch, no one feels alone.

The vines twist, telling stories bold,
Of secret seeds and leaves of gold.
With every breeze, a laugh does bloom,
In this garden, joy finds room.

Cadence of the Canopied Realm

In a forest where trees wear hats,
Squirrels gossip, sharing chats.
The branches play a tune so bright,
As shadows dance in morning light.

Beneath the canopy of cheer,
The owls wink, spreading good cheer.
Frogs croak silly serenades,
While crickets make dance parades.

A bear tries on a comical grin,
While raccoons join the fun with a spin.
The leaves rustle in laughter loud,
As nature gathers quite a crowd.

With every rustle, stories weave,
In this realm, it's hard to believe.
Where laughter blooms from root to crown,
And smiles bounce up like butterflies down.

Sonnet of the Swaying Sorrel

Oh, sorrel swaying in the breeze,
Tickling noses with humor's tease.
With every gust, a giggle stirs,
As dandelions tease with purrs.

The bees buzz with a ticklish tone,
Joking about their honeyed throne.
While sorrel whispers, "What's the fuss?"
"Just watch the carrots make a fuss!"

Though the sun may bask and glow,
It's laughter that helps friendships grow.
In patches green, the fun unfolds,
With tales of nutty mushrooms told.

So dance, dear sorrel, sway and swirl,
In the garden's laugh, let joy unfurl.
Each leaf a chuckle, each root a rhyme,
Nature's comedy stands the test of time.

Ballad of the Burgeoning Boughs

Oh boughs that stretch with playful grace,
In the sunlight, a merry chase.
Treetops tickle clouds above,
As nature winks, filled with love.

The breeze plays tricks on every leaf,
Whispering secrets without grief.
Branches lean in for a chat,
While squirrels bounce around like that!

Underneath, the critters play
A game of tag, hip-hip-hooray!
Mice hold parties on the ground,
While laughter echoes all around.

With every rustle, joy ignites,
As shadows dance on sunny nights.
In this grove, the world feels bright,
With burgeoning boughs in pure delight.

Chronicles of the Clovers

In a patch where the clovers play,
A grasshopper dances, hip-hip-hooray!
Telling tales of the bees in a buzz,
While ants all march, as they always does.

The sun peeks down with a cheeky grin,
While worms in the soil are plotting to win,
A treasure of snacks hidden so sweet,
While squirrels scamper on tiny, fast feet.

With giggles of daisies, so fresh and bright,
Joking with spiders that weave with delight,
The frogs all jump in a puddle so grand,
Creating a splash that's simply unplanned.

So gather your laughter, and let's take a look,
In the green of the field where nature's the book,
Each chapter a chuckle, a jest with a twist,
In the chronicles where fun can't be missed.

Harmonies of the Heights

Up in the trees where the high winds blow,
A parrot sings tunes in a colorful show,
He's got moves that would make dancers gleam,
While squirrels applaud, with a nutty scream.

The clouds are bopping in rhythm so fine,
While a fox in the shade sips on some brine,
The sunlight flickers, a spotlight of cheer,
As owls keep hooting, pretending to hear.

With laughter from branches, the leaves join the mix,
While a raccoon juggles with shiny tricks,
The harmony rises, a hilarious sight,
In the heights where the critters unite with delight.

So dance with the breeze, and sway to the sound,
Let merriment echo through forest profound,
Every note is a giggle, each rustle a jest,
In the heights where all creatures just love to fest.

Dialogues with the Daisies

In a meadow bright, with daisies so chatty,
They gossip and giggle, they can be quite batty,
"Did you see the butterfly's flashy new dress?"
"Oh, darling, it's fab, it's simply the best!"

A ladybug joins with a wink and a wave,
Sharing secrets of how she's so brave,
"Did you hear about that snail's slow escapade?"
"Oh yes, but it's better with some lemonade!"

The daisies debate about fashion and flair,
While ants pass around their snack in the air,
The grass grows tall, it sways to the tune,
While the sun winks in, "Catch me later at noon!"

Their dialogues flourish throughout the day,
With laughter and stories, in their own quirky way,
So stop by the patch for a chat and a cheer,
With the daisies who offer such joy through the year.

Echoing in the Earth's Embrace

In the warm embrace where the critters dwell,
A gopher's got jokes, he knows them so well,
He burrows a tunnel with punchlines galore,
"Why did the chicken? To hop through the door!"

The laughter ripples through roots far and wide,
While a mischievous mole takes a comedic slide,
The earth seems to chuckle, it trembles with glee,
As earthworms join in, singing, "Let it be free!"

In caverns and caves, the echoes resound,
With humor alive in the underground,
A party of fungi, both quirky and round,
Join in the fun with mycelium sound.

So giggle with critters, feel joy as it flows,
In the earth's sweet embrace, where laughter just grows,
With every hearty chuckle, and each fun-filled tease,
Let the echoes of nature put all minds at ease.

Refrains in the Rain

Puddles splashed with every step,
Jumping high, we squeal and prep.
Raindrops dance like tiny folks,
Laughing loudly with the jokes.

Umbrellas turn to boats, oh dear,
Sailing puddles without fear.
Ducks in coats hold court and quack,
As we slide down the wet grass track.

The skies might frown, but we won't care,
We'll twirl and swirl in rain-soaked air.
With squishy shoes and giggles bright,
We claim the storm; we're birds in flight.

So let it pour, let thunder roll,
We've found our groove; we've found our goal.
A bashful sun peeks through the gray,
We'll dance in rain 'til close of day.

Sonnet of the Sedge

In grassy beds where strange things grow,
The frogs will croak, and worms will show.
Sedges tug at socks like mad,
While wind whispers secrets, oh so glad.

A rabbit hops, he thinks he's sly,
But stumbles on a butterfly.
With laughter shared as they collide,
The blooms all giggle, hearts open wide.

Beetles roll their favorite dice,
Playing tricks and tossing spice.
The sun winks down, a cheeky light,
As nature's court claims day and night.

So join the game, don't be too shy,
With nature's jest, we'll laugh and fly.
In fields of whimsy, joy is found,
Where silly dances spin around.

Melodies from the Meadowlark

A lark sings tunes from high up there,
Where daisies nod and bumblebees stare.
With melodies that weave through air,
The hillsides echo, oh what a flair!

Ants march along with tiny feet,
In a conga line, oh what a feat!
Grasshoppers leap in a playful game,
While ladybugs boast their polka-dots' fame.

The tulips sway, they've got the beat,
They know the steps; they move their sweet.
With sunshine streaming, it's a show,
Nature's party is all aglow!

So come and sing, join in the fun,
Under the rays of a golden sun.
With laughter loud and hearts so free,
In the meadow, be wild and glee!

Verse Beneath the Vine

Beneath the vine, the worlds collide,
With grapes a-grinning, side by side.
They whisper tales of juice and cheer,
As giggles roll, the way is clear.

A squirrel tightrope-walks the line,
With acorns clutched, oh so divine.
He'll flip and flop, a comical scene,
As birds applaud, all bright and green.

The wind joins in, a playful tease,
Ruffling leaves like a gentle breeze.
Nature's circus with critters spry,
A show so grand, it makes you sigh!

So grab a seat where laughter's sewn,
Among the vines, you'll feel right at home.
With friends around and sun so fine,
We'll cheer for joy, beneath the vine.

Tones of the Turquoise Lake

Ducks in sunglasses float on by,
They quack a tune, oh me, oh my!
Fish in the depths do a silly dance,
While frogs in the reeds join in the prance.

A turtle hums with a wink and a smile,
Singing to lizards, they groove for a while.
Splash of colors as the sun goes down,
Who knew the lake could hold such a clown?

Prose in the Petal Pile

A bumblebee scribbles tales of delight,
In a garden where blossoms take flight.
With petals like pages that flutter and sway,
They borrow the wind to share what they say.

The daisies gossip with vibrant glee,
While dandelions dance, wild and free.
Sunflowers laugh, their heads held high,
While roses roll on, refusing to cry.

Cadence in the Cornucopia

In a basket where veggies jam and groove,
Cabbages twirl, trying to prove.
Tomatoes giggle, so plump and red,
As radishes shout that they're already fed.

Garlic tells stories, smoky and bold,
While carrots exchange their secrets of gold.
In this feast of laughter, they create a song,
A melody that just can't be wrong!

Reflections in the Rooted Realm

Beneath the soil where the giggles grow,
The worms host a party—what a show!
With turns and twists in the earthy ground,
They wiggle and writhe, oh what a sound!

The beetles compete in a silly race,
While moles wear hats, adding to the pace.
Roots laugh together, tickled by the rain,
In a world where silliness is never in vain.

Harmonies of the Hidden Flora

In the garden where gnomes dance,
The tomatoes fancy a chance.
They twirl in their vines all day,
Whispering secrets in a playful way.

The daisies giggle, so bright and bold,
Telling the tales of fairies and gold.
While the weeds plot to break the fun,
They'll trip on each other 'til day is done.

The carrots wear hats, so stylish and neat,
Peppers hum tunes, a juicy beat.
With spinach so strong, it flexes with pride,
While onions look sly, all teary-eyed.

So come to the realm of nature's jest,
Where roots come alive, and laughter's the best.
The blooms trade jokes while they sway and spin,
In the hidden world where the fun begins.

Stanzas in the Soil

Beneath the earth, a party's in store,
With worms that groove and beetles that soar.
Potatoes joke about their round, starchy lives,
While the broccoli broods where no sunlight thrives.

The mushrooms play tricks, with caps all aglow,
Telling the daisies where not to go.
The clovers roll dice, in hopes of a win,
Cheering for rain to make the fun spin.

The radishes chuckle, so rad and so red,
While grassy green sprouts lie quietly spread.
Each root shares a laugh, though buried away,
As tiny ants march, in their own silly sway.

In this patchwork terrain of humorous flights,
The soil's a stage for fresh, funny sights.
So dig in the dirt, and you just might find,
A giggle or two, left behind by the kind.

Poetic Paths of the Underbrush

In thickets where creatures play hide and seek,
The bushes are whispering, and branches sneak.
A squirrel in jest, wears a nutty disguise,
While the foxes share riddles, oh what a surprise.

A hedgehog rolls in, spiky and round,
He trips on a twig, tumbling down to the ground.
The rabbits are giggling, with twitches so slight,
As they hop and they skip in the soft moonlight.

The grasses are nodding, so playful and spry,
A chorus of chirps sends the crickets up high.
With daisies and clovers in a merry parade,
The underbrush dances, a whimsical charade.

So venture and wander on paths made of fun,
Where laughter grows wild, under moon and sun.
For the stories untold mingle deep in the shade,
In the heart of the forest where music is played.

Lullabies of the Leafy Realm

At dusk in the woods, the leaves start to hum,
A lullaby sweet, as the critters all come.
The ferns wiggle softly, in a sleepy embrace,
While the owls spin tales, with a wise, silly grace.

The fireflies twinkle, like stars in the fray,
Bidding farewell to the end of the day.
A chipmunk with cookies, all crunched and chewed,
Makes bedtime a banquet, in woods' cozy mood.

The branches sway gently, in rhythm divine,
While the crickets compose, with a thin, twinkling line.
Each whispering rustle is a soft, loving song,
As the leafy realm hums, where we all belong.

So nestle in close, let the night bear your dreams,
In the garden of giggles, where nothing is as it seems.
For here in the twilight, with friends nestled tight,
The lullabies linger, until morning light.

The Song of the Sprouting Seed

In the soil, a seedling grins,
It wiggles and shakes, and then spins.
A worm passes by with a jest,
"You're sprouting up fast! Aren't you blessed?"

The raindrops dance on the ground,
A puddle forms, oh what fun is found!
The sun beams down with a cheeky smile,
"Grow big, little friend, it's your style!"

Leaves pop out, waving with glee,
"Look at us, we're a leafy spree!"
The ants march by in fancy shoes,
"A dance party here? We cannot refuse!"

With roots deep down and branches up high,
The sprout dreams of touching the sky.
It hums a tune from its little heart,
"Let's all grow wild, let's make art!"

Litany of the Leafy Labyrinth

In a maze of leaves, I lose my way,
A squirrel chuckles, in grand display.
"Who knew these greens could play such tricks?"
His acorn stash is hidden in sticks!

A vine wraps round like a playful friend,
"Come take the path where the laughter blends!"
I zigzag here, I twirl around,
While daisies giggle on the ground.

The sun peeks in with a wink so bright,
A butterfly flutters, spreading delight.
"Please do stay, don't rush away,"
"There's so much fun in this leafy ballet!"

As shadows dance, the day slips away,
"Let's make a wish, let's laugh and play!"
In this leafy maze, I'll always roam,
With chuckles and giggles, I feel at home.

Harmonious Heights of the Hedges

In hedges high, a songbird sings,
While hedgehogs bounce, oh, what joy springs!
A chorus of crickets join the beat,
With every note, they tap their feet.

The rabbits hop with a cheerful cheer,
"Let's gather round, a banquet here!"
With carrots, peas, and berries so sweet,
They munch and crunch to the rhythmic beat.

A breeze whispers through the leaves so green,
Carrying tunes of the unseen.
As the hedges sway and dance in delight,
Let's party till the stars are bright!

At sunset's glow, the fun won't cease,
The garden's alive, filled with peace.
With laughter abounding and joy in the air,
In this hedge of wonder, there's love to share!

The Tune of Treetop Tales

Up in the treetops, stories unfold,
With monkeys swinging, so bold and cold.
"Swing with us high, we'll touch the stars!"
Squeals of joy outshine the cars.

The leaves whisper secrets, a playful tease,
As squirrels giggle in the gentle breeze.
With every branch a tale is spun,
"Come join our fun, don't let it shun!"

The moon peeks through with a knowing grin,
"Atop these trees, let the tales begin!"
With owls hooting a curious pitch,
They gather 'round, igniting the switch.

From heights above, the laughter rings,
Nature's magic, oh, how it sings!
With twinkling dreams and stories so bright,
In treetop tales, we find pure delight!

Sonnet of the Silvers

In the garden where the critters play,
A silver squirrel stole my snack today.
He did a dance, a jig so spry,
With acorns flying, oh my, oh my!

The sun shone bright, the leaves did cheer,
As he flipped and flopped without any fear.
I laughed so hard, nearly fell off my seat,
That wild little rascal, light on his feet!

But then came the crow, with a caw so loud,
Chasing the squirrel, drawing a crowd.
With a flap and a flurry, they dashed up the bark,
A comical chase, a true work of art!

So here's to the critters that dance and they prance,
With twirls and swirls, they take every chance.
In this crazy triangle of laughter and fun,
Our garden's a circus, the show's just begun!

Reverberations from the Roots

Deep in the soil, where the earthworms groove,
The roots tell stories, with a silly move.
They wiggle and tickle, causing a stir,
Planting their jokes, oh how they concur!

Frogs in the pond, they croak out a tune,
While mushrooms join in, they're over the moon!
Together they bellow, a raucous delight,
In harmony hidden, beneath day and night.

The gnomes join the fun, with their hats so tall,
Playing on banjos, a marvelous hall.
As laughter erupts from roots deep below,
All nature's in on it, putting on a show!

So listen real close to the whispers they share,
In the laughter of roots, you'll find love and care.
With giggles and snickers, the earth spins around,
In this comical chorus, joy knows no bound!

Tones in the Treetops

Up in the branches, the parakeets sing,
Kazoos in their beaks, it's a quirky thing!
With each silly note, they flap and they sway,
They've got rhythm and moves that just slay!

The wind starts to whistle, joining their song,
As the trees do a shimmy, all day long.
Leaves clap their hands in a rustling cheer,
Celebrating nature's own band of the year!

A raccoon on a branch, he's tapping his feet,
While owls hoot along, with a beat that's sweet.
Together they giggle in this woodland jubilee,
Creating a symphony, happy and free!

So look to the treetops, where the laughter flies,
With notes that are silly, and giggles that rise.
In this leafy concert, joy takes its flight,
Under the canopy, everything feels right!

Melody of the Mould

In the corners of the garden, where the mushrooms sprout,

A moldy mischief dances about.
With a twirl and a twist, the spores take the floor,
Chasing each other, for fun they implore!

The slugs slide in with a slimy ballet,
While the beetles click-clack, they're starting to play.
Together they frolic, in a fungus-filled spree,
Making melodies, just wait and see!

A breeze brings the laughter, spreading the cheer,
As the compost joins in, it's a party, oh dear!
Terracotta pots and the snazzy old bricks,
Form the whole orchestra with all of their tricks!

So if you wander near, stop for a tune,
The symphony's hidden, beneath the full moon.
In this patch of delight, with laughter that's bold,
Is the sweet melody of the marvelous mould!

Chants of the Cypress

In a forest where trees dance and sway,
The cypress writes poems in a humorous way.
With needles for quills, they scribble all night,
While squirrels recite them with sheer delight.

The owls hoot giggles, the foxes all cheer,
As laughter spreads out, from root to frontier.
Branches bend lower, embracing the prank,
A party for critters down at the bank.

A chorus of critters, no worries to find,
In the shade of the cypress, the joy is unconfined.
Frogs leap in rhythm, the bugs join the tune,
It's an uproar of fun beneath the full moon.

So, here's to the cypress, the joker of trees,
With each playful twist of a warm summer breeze.
No serious business, just laughter and glee,
In the heart of the forest, forever carefree.

Odes to the Oaken Old

Oh, the old oak stands tall with a mischievous grin,
Telling tales of his youth as he wiggles a limb.
His acorns are jokes that he drops with a thud,
And all of his friends are just rolling in mud.

He whispers sweet secrets to leaves in the air,
To the squirrels collecting their nutty affair.
With laughter he rustles his branches so wide,
Challenging birds to a comedic ride.

The mighty oak chuckles, his trunk full of cheer,
He plays hide and seek with the chipmunks so near.
Each ring in his bark is a punchline well-crafted,
In the grand show of life, he is happily drafted.

So, let's raise a toast to the old oak today,
For all of his jests in the sun's golden ray.
With leaves all a-shimmer, he knows how to jest,
Bringing giggles to all, he truly is best.

Lyricism of the Lichen

On rocks and on trees, where the lichen does grow,
It sings silly songs in a hush and a glow.
With spots full of color, it jokes all around,
Creating a festival right on the ground.

Mosses join in with a soft, fuzzy sound,
While mushrooms tap dance in a circle unbound.
The forest's a stage for this curious show,
In a world where delight is set free to bestow.

Lichen brings humor to pockets of light,
As critters pass by, giggling in flight.
Its charm is contagious, it spreads without shame,
As the owl in the branches whispers its name.

So, let's paint the forest with laughter and cheer,
For the lichen brings whimsy whenever it's near.
In nature's own harmony, let joy be the gift,
As the world turns to laughter, our spirits will lift.

Symphony of the Shrubs

In the thicket of shrubs, there's a cacophony bright,
Where laughter erupts, bringing joy and delight.
With branches a-bouncing and leaves made of glee,
The shrubs hold a concert for all creatures free.

Berries join in with a high-pitched cheer,
While crickets strum songs that the birds hold dear.
Each rustle and giggle makes whispers ignite,
As the blooms throw a party that lasts through the night.

The frogs croak a melody, the bees hum along,
It's a shrubbery symphony, lively and strong.
With laughter like petals that flutter and sway,
Turning moments of quiet into a bright ballet.

So here in the shrubs, let's dance and let loose,
For the symphony's got us, it's time to cut loose.
With joy intertwining, our spirits will soar,
In the orchestra of laughter, we will forever explore.

Echoes of the Earth

Beneath the soil where worms wriggle,
The trees listen and start to giggle.
A squirrel hops, then takes a dive,
Yelling, "Hey, I'm still alive!"

The stones all chuckle as they lay,
At passing ants that dance and sway.
With roots that tickle, they mock the air,
Whispering jokes without a care.

Verses Beneath the Canopy

Under the leaves, the shadows play,
A raccoon breaks in with a bold display.
"Why join the circus?" he questions quite sly,
"Because the trunk's the best place to fly!"

The mushrooms giggle, their caps all aglow,
As laughter ripples through the roots below.
Fungi share tales of a dance long past,
"Let's thump the ground, make this party last!"

Whispered Words of the Wilderness

In a thicket where the lilacs bloom,
A fox tells tales of impending doom.
"I saw a dog running through the glade,
With one shoe on, he looked quite afraid!"

The bushes rustle, as critters conspire,
Their secret giggles catch the wind like fire.
"Let's throw a feast! We'll bring the snacks!
But keep it quiet, or we'll attract the tax!"

Melody of the Subterranean

Beneath the ground, where secrets twirl,
A gopher pipes up, "Wait, what's that swirl?"
"My cheese stash has been raided," he cries,
"Who's stealing snacks? It's no surprise!"

The moles all nod with a knowing grin,
"Must've been the badger, he's always in!"
They plan a heist, with hats and capes,
To reclaim their goodies, with cheeky shapes!

Anthem of the Aspens

In a grove of whispers, trees do sway,
Leaves like giggles, they dance and play.
Branches stretch wide, in silly glee,
Barking out jokes, just like a spree.

They chuckle in sun, then snicker in rain,
Aspens debate who's lost a chain.
Roots tickle the ground, in a playful tease,
Sharing their secrets with every breeze.

With rustling laughter, the shadows blend,
Each twig a story, it twists, it bends.
Roots set the stage for this lively show,
Where jokes grow tall, and the punchlines flow.

When winter comes knocking, they shiver and freeze,
The jokes hibernate, with the greatest of ease.
But spring brings a riot, of green and jest,
Aspens unite for their comedy fest.

Tapestry of the Timberline

At the edge of the hill, where the fun never quits,
Timberlines gather for their comedy skits.
Pines wear their hats, spruce find their shoes,
All in the mood to chuckle and muse.

Moss laughs in green, as the branches chime,
Stumpy old trunks tell jokes out of rhyme.
The wildflowers giggle, dressed in a swirl,
As saplings drop puns like a pearl in a whirl.

Beneath all the laughter, there's fun underground,
Roots tickle their neighbors, with giggles abound.
Tap on the bark, hear a smile take flight,
Under the quilt of the stars at night.

With every tall tale that these trees do weave,
They cheer up the clouds, make the raindrops believe.
So join in the chorus of rustles and tunes,
As the Timberline shimmers beneath the full moons.

Songs of the Seasons

In springtime's embrace, the buds burst with cheer,
Barking out humor, the blooms persevere.
Squirrels chime in with their cheeky retorts,
While bumblebees buzz just cracking the sorts.

Summer rolls in, with sunburnt delights,
Leaves often gossip about past winter nights.
The winds carry tales, like ships to the shore,
Each rustle a laugh, each gust leaves them wanting more.

Autumn alights in costumes so bold,
With scarves full of color and stories retold.
Trees trade their treasures, with laughter to share,
Recounting the frolics of creatures they dare.

Winter, though frigid, brings silliness still,
Icicles jingle, with a chill and a thrill.
They huddle together, in their snowy-clad boots,
And chuckle at snowflakes in comical suits.

Echoing through the Coral

In a reef of colors, where the fish have a ball,
Coral makes music with a giggle and call.
Seaweed does tickle, as currents pass by,
While clams share their secrets with a wink and a sigh.

Jellyfish jump like they're in a parade,
With tentacles jiving, a dance they have made.
Anemones giggle, giving glow-in-the-dark,
Playing peek-a-boo under sunrays so stark.

The crabs tell tall tales, with claws waving wide,
As octopuses chuckle, their ink spots like pride.
Bubbles float upward, in a whimsical race,
Each one a tickle, a smile on the face.

The ocean laughs loud, echoing glee,
In the coral's embrace, so wild and free.
With each swish and swirl, comedies bloom,
Making ripples of joy in the watery room.

Secrets of the Soil

The worms hold secrets, they wiggle and squirm,
Their gossip is juicy, it makes the earth warm.
They shout to the beetles, they whisper to bees,
"Dig deeper, my friend, more treasure to seize!"

In shadows, the radish will crack a sly grin,
While carrots root down, with their orange kin.
The daisies will giggle, the daisies will sway,
As cabbage rolls out, to join in the play.

Oh cabbage, dear cabbage, you think you're so cool,
But up in the garden, it's quite the wild school!
With lettuce debating, and peas in a row,
They're planning a party for all of the show!

So when you walk by, take heed of the soil,
For under your feet, there's laughter and toil.
With roots intertwining in a dance so neat,
You'll find that the plants have their own little beat.

Verses in the Vineyard

The grapes are all bouncing, they're having a ball,
With stems all a-twisting, they party so tall.
They toast with their skins, make juice for a cheer,
"Let's ferment this joy, we've nothing to fear!"

The vines tell a tale, with a twist and a turn,
As they climb up the trellis, and wait for their learn.
Red, white, and bubbly, they giggle with glee,
"Here's to our next batch, let's make it a spree!"

With sunlight a-dancing on leaves in repose,
The grapes share their secrets and tickle their toes.
They whisper of flavors, of earthy delights,
With laughter that sparkles like stars in the nights.

So pass by the vineyards, let laughter abide,
As grapes raise a glass, with the sun as their guide.
In the rhythm of harvest, they're songs that resound,
In verses so sweet, with joy all around.

Cadence of the Canopy

High above our heads, the branches do sway,
They wave to the sunlight, they dance in the play.
The leaves form a chorus, a rustling sound,
As critters join in, with their footsteps around.

The squirrels are the jesters, so cheeky and spry,
They throw acorns like confetti, oh my, oh my!
With a leap and a bound, they tumble and roll,
Creating a pub, right at nature's soul.

The owls hoot in rhythm, a wise serenade,
While insects can't help but dance in the shade.
A waltz in the branches, a jig in the breeze,
It's music afoot, in the rustle of trees.

So listen up closely, when walking below,
The canopy sings, with a world full of glow.
With laughter and giggles, a forest so grand,
The branches unite, in a whimsical band.

Stanzas in the Shadows

In the shade of the trees, the secrets are spun,
Where shadows are dancers, and sunlight's the fun.
The toads croak out stanzas, so silly and sweet,
While fireflies flicker, a rhythmic heartbeat.

The mushrooms are poets, they giggle and grow,
With caps like umbrellas, they put on a show.
They whisper soft verses, in a delicate trance,
And invite all the critters to join in their dance.

The breeze tells a story, a chuckle or two,
While the grasshoppers join in on the lyrical crew.
They bounce with a cadence, from leaf to the ground,
In a joyful performance, with friends all around.

So wander the shadows, where laughter is found,
In stanzas of silliness, nature astounds.
Where every small creature has a tale to write,
In the playful dim air, they sing through the night.

Symphony of the Subterranean

In the soil where worms do dance,
They twirl and spin without a chance.
They hold a concert underground,
With squeaky shoes, they make a sound.

The moles are drummers, rocks their stage,
The ants all cheer, they're quite the page.
But when the gophers join the show,
The whole ensemble starts to grow.

Beneath the roots, where giggles play,
The beetles crawl in wild ballet.
A rooty tune with beats so shy,
As mischief lurks with every sigh.

So join this group of laugh and cheer,
The underground's the place to steer.
When roots combine with tales and glee,
A funny world of roots you'll see.

Odes to the Olive Grove

The olives laugh on branches high,
With wrinkled skins, they wink and sigh.
They tell a tale of sunny days,
And squeaky laughter in sun's rays.

A squirrel slips, a branch gives way,
It grunts and squeals, a clumsy play.
The olives chuckle, roll and sway,
While robins sing the joy of May.

The breeze is carrying a tune,
A harmony beneath the moon.
Each olive sings of days gone by,
While leafy friends hum in reply.

So raise a glass of olive cheer,
For funny tales of those held dear.
In groves of joy, we find delight,
With every laugh that takes its flight.

Lyrics of the Landscape

The hills have hats made out of grass,
They tip their brims as you walk past.
With laughter caught in swirling breeze,
Each leaf is dancing with such ease.

The rocks, they gossip, oh so sly,
With stories that make daisies pry.
The rivers giggle and will swirl,
While frogs perform a funny twirl.

Clouds wear shoes of fluffy white,
And stomp around without a fright.
Each mountain echoes friendly fun,
As if the earth is full of pun.

So roam the hills and laugh out loud,
As nature makes a vibrant crowd.
With every step upon this lace,
You'll find a smile in every place.

Chants of the Chasm

Deep in the chasm, echoes sing,
Of frogs who hop and birds on wing.
They chant a tune of funny fate,
Where shadows dance and giggles wait.

The crevice holds a party bright,
With rocks that twinkle in the night.
The laughter twirls, a joyous mix,
As crickets play their silly tricks.

The walls, they clap with echoes loud,
While each new jest draws in a crowd.
A bouncing ball of fun and cheer,
In caverns deep, we've no more fear.

So visit where the laughter flows,
In chasms deep, the funny grows.
With every chant from stones and breeze,
A giggling world, a heart that frees.

Paean of the Pollen

The bees in the breeze seem to dance with delight,
With a buzz and a whirr, they take off in flight.
They sip from the flowers, their tiny, sweet feast,
Spreading joy all around, like a pollen-filled beast.

Oh, the dandelions laugh as they puff out their fluff,
While the clover gets giggly when the sun gets too tough.
Each petal a riddle, each stamen a prank,
Nature's own jokes, poured out from a tank.

Hymn of the Herbaceous Haunt

The sage sings a tune, oh what a wild sight,
With rosemary twirling, they dance into night.
Thyme's feeling cheeky, throws in a sly wink,
While basil starts plotting, and spinach begins to rethink.

Mint's green giggles echo, a prankster galore,
While parsley gives side-eyes, whose roots are a bore.
Chives chuckle softly, with a snicker and sigh,
Herbs in a frenzy, oh my, oh my!

Cacophony of the Canes

The bamboo stands bold, with a creaky old song,
As the wind blows through, it just can't go wrong.
With a sway and a nod, they plot mischief anew,
The tall grass is laughing, and the bushes join too.

Those canes have a party, a bash up the hill,
With the squirrels as guests — such a rascally thrill!
They chatter and chatter, a wild, funny crew,
With jokes about acorns and how to catch dew.

Echoing Enchantment of the Earth

The roots play a game in their underground zone,
With tickles and whispers, they're never alone.
A gopher dives deep, with a goofy old grin,
While mushrooms are giggling, saying, 'Let's begin!'

Worms wiggle in rhythm, a sassy old dance,
While the stones start to rumble, 'Give nature a chance!'
Through laughter and coziness, joy fills the ground,
In this earthy embrace, happiness is found.

Chords of the Gnarled Growth

In the forest where the branches sway,
A squirrel's mischief brightens the day.
With acorns flying, he takes his shot,
For who knew trees could be that distraught?

The owls chuckle, hooting their jest,
As raccoons play tug-of-war with a vest.
The pine trees sway with a creaky laugh,
Finding humor in their crooked half.

A badger hums an off-key tune,
While frogs croak along, a wild cartoon.
The thorns prickle, tickling all around,
Nature's chorus, strange and profound.

So here's to laughter in nature's lot,
With saplings prancing in a happy plot.
Let's celebrate life with joy and cheer,
For even in silence, laughter draws near.

Tones from the Twisting Tendrils

In the garden where the weeds play,
A broccoli dressed like a cabaret.
Carrots dancing with their orange flair,
While radishes giggle in the air.

Oh, the daisies spin around in glee,
Talking gossip with a bumblebee.
The lettuce whispers jokes on the vine,
While potatoes dream of sipping wine.

Cucumbers hide in their leafy beds,
Daring the turnips to clash their heads.
Tomatoes chuckle as they turn red,
Creating chaos while dreaming of bread.

So let us laugh with our plants at night,
In the moon's glow, they twirl with delight.
Nature's humor, a jolly parade,
As the garden sings, none are afraid.

Flourishing Footsteps in Verse

In the meadow where the daisies blaze,
Frogs practice leaps in a hop-filled craze.
With crickets strumming their tiny strings,
Every step bursts forth with zany flings.

Bees do a dance, so wild and spry,
While butterflies flutter, asking why.
The sunflowers twist, heads held high,
As they join in with a wink and a sigh.

Little ants march in perfect file,
Wearing tiny hats, oh what a style!
Each step a jig, as they scuttle about,
Making the world happy without a doubt.

So let's clap hands for this lively scene,
Where every plant is a comic machine.
In the meadow of mirth, let's sing and prance,
For life's a joke in a playful dance.

Meter Beneath the Meadow

In the meadow where the grasses sway,
A rabbit trips on his own ballet.
He shakes his head, then hops with flair,
While clouds giggle, floating in air.

Butterflies waltz, wings all aglow,
Wishing the flowers could dance just so.
Caterpillars in a conga line,
Twisting and turning, feeling divine.

The whispers of daisies, a playful tease,
As bunnies nibble with utmost ease.
With each snicker, the world comes alive,
Amidst the rows where the wild things thrive.

So let's join in on this frolicsome beat,
In fields of laughter, life is complete.
For in each giggle sprouting from ground,
The heartbeat of nature's joy is found.

www.ingramcontent.com/pod-product-compliance
Lightning Source LLC
Chambersburg PA
CBHW051639160426
43209CB00004B/712